Clear round Rach

ISBN 978-1-905184-29-3

All illustrations by Ian Cryer

Not very long ago, before motorways, fast cars, fast food and computers, thousands of horses worked on the railway, moving millions of tons of goods every year. This is the second of a series of stories about just one of them, Rachael.

Ian Cryer

Designed by Paul Karau
Printed by Amadeus Press Ltd., Cleckheaton

Published by
WILD SWAN PUBLICATIONS LTD.
1-3 Hagbourne Road, Didcot, Oxon, OX11 8DP

Rachael

the Railway Horse

By Ian Cryer

Clear round Rachael

LEWIS

Rachael the Railway Horse, Carter Jack and Toby were out working in the town, it was Saturday morning and they were all looking forward to the weekend break; it had been a long busy week.

At around 10 o'clock they passed a field where a Show Jumping competition was about to begin. Rachael saw the horses practising prior to the start of the show. They looked excited as their proud owners prepared them for the challenge ahead.

The trio carried on down the road to the next drop. Rachael stood thinking about the show jumpers while Carter Jack made another delivery. "I wish I could have some fun for a change instead of just pulling this van around all the time", thought Rachael.

On the way back to the yard Carter Jack noticed that Rachael seemed a bit down. "Cheer up my girl" said Carter Jack, but Rachael still seemed low. "I'll tell you what we'll do, Rachael" said Carter Jack. "Before we go back to the stable, we'll stop on the grass verge by the railway line and you can have some fresh grass". Rachael's spirit lifted immediately and she trotted along happily.

True to his word, Carter Jack stopped the van and unhitched Rachael. "There we are, my girl" he said, "tuck in to that tasty grass. I'll even take off your bridle so you can eat more comfortably." Rachael munched happily on the fresh spring grass, it was a nice change from the dry feed she normally had back at the stable.

A goods train appeared in the distance and slowly made its way towards the signal that stood next to the little group. "That train's going to be held at the signal" said Carter Jack. "I wonder if Rachael will be bothered by the engine hissing."

The train pulled up alongside Rachael but she took no notice. She had seen plenty of engines before and she carried on eating. “Hello, Carter Jack,” shouted the driver, ‘how are you? I haven’t seen you for ages, come up and have a chat and a cup of tea.” Carter Jack grabbed his tin mug and made his way up the bank to the engine.

Carter Jack stood on the footplate of the engine chatting with his old friend Driver Watts. "We might be here for a while waiting for the late-running Express to pass." he explained. "I'm in no hurry" said Carter Jack, "I've finished my deliveries and Rachael's quite happy enjoying that fresh grass."

The old friends were engrossed in conversation and forgot that the boiler pressure on the engine was creeping up. "Here comes the express at last," said Driver Watts. "In good time too" added the Fireman, pointing at the steam gauge, "as the safety valve is about to blow". "What!" shouted Carter Jack, "I'd better get back to Rachael, I don't think she's ever been next to an engine when it's blowing off!"

Carter Jack hurried off the engine and down the bank, tumbling over in his panic, just as the Express train thundered past, trailing smoke and steam down the line. The carriage wheels clattered over the rail joints, 'Dadung Dadung, Dadung Dadung'.

He ran over to Rachael to reassure her and tell her not to be frightened by the impending noise, but it was too late. There was a deafening blast as steam shot out of the safety valve, high into the air. Rachael reared up on her hind legs, snapping her lead rope, terrified by the ear-piercing din. Carter Jack grabbed hold of Rachael's harness to try to control her.

But Rachael charged down the street, with Carter Jack hanging on for dear life, pursued by Toby. People jumped for cover as the terrified horse bounded along. The road cleared ahead, but at the end of the road was a fence. "Oh no! we're going to hit the fence" cried Carter Jack.

W

Carter Jack closed his eyes, fearing the worst, but Rachael suddenly took to the air, gliding over the fence and into the show-jumping field. There were hundreds of people ahead watching the show, but Rachael spotted an opening in the crowd.

The commentator was just announcing that none of the competitors had achieved a clear round, when Rachael burst into the ring with Carter Jack still hanging on precariously. "But wait," said the Commentator, "we appear to have a late entry, I think it's that grey mare from the railway yard."

Rachael was in a blind panic when a jump appeared in front of her. Without thinking, Rachael took to the air again. As she hit the ground on the other side, the crowd started to cheer. "Go on, Rachael" they bellowed.

Carter Jack had no control but managed to land upright on Rachael's back. The commentator was full of praise, "Look at this magnificent display of horsemanship, Carter Jack is riding without a rein or even a proper saddle." Rachael took on fence after fence but then the crowd went quiet as she approached the final and most difficult hurdle.

In complete silence, she took a breath and launched herself at the mighty wall; as she glided over, one of Rachael's hoofs just clipped a block, for a moment it teetered precariously, but stayed in place. The crowd went wild as Rachael touched down and headed for the finish line.

Rachael at last pulled up, but so sharply that Carter Jack tumbled forward and crashed to the ground in front of Rachael. Carter Jack went bright red with embarrassment, thinking he had shown himself up in front of all those people. But they were soon surrounded by a very happy and excited crowd.

Regaining their composure, the unexpected champions were presented with the winner's rosette by the chief Judge, Lady Cynthia Bonneville-Holmes. "Many congratulations, Carter Jack and Rachael, yours was the only clear round and achieved in record time." Carter Jack accepted the honour with a wry smile and said nothing. Rachael looked very pleased with herself but the other horses looked on in disgust at the thought of having been beaten by a carthorse!

Back at the station, Carter Jack told his tale. "I don't believe you" said Pete the Porter, "and you should know, Rule 57 clearly states that under no circumstances are company horses to be entered into show jumping or cross-country competitions."

"But we didn't enter", argued Carter Jack, "it just happened."

"Well if it did just happen", continued Pete the Porter, "I should keep quiet about it in case Mr Gorman the Foreman finds out or you'll be in for the high jump as well as Rachael!"

"Oh, it did happen, Pete the Porter" insisted Miss Park the Cartage Clerk, "I was there, they were fantastic".

Mr Gorman the Foreman then appeared on the scene. Carter Jack quickly hid the rosette behind his back. “How did you get on with your morning round, Carter Jack?” he enquired.

“Very well” answered Carter Jack, “you could say we had a Clear Round, didn’t we Rachael!” Pete the Porter and Miss Park the Cartage Clerk fell about laughing, but Mr Gorman looked bemused. He didn’t get the joke!

Other stories in the Rachael the Railway Horse series:

RACHAEL'S FIRST DAY

This first book tells the story of Rachael's first day of working for the Great Western Railway and introduces the characters who become part of her everyday life.

ISBN 978-1-905184-26-2 (hardback)
ISBN 978-1-905184-27-9 (cardback)

MONKEY BUSINESS

Monkeys cause havoc while being transported to the zoo. A lengthy chase ensues after they hijack the banana special train but their greed proves to be their undoing.

www.rachaeltherailwayhorse.com